Hawaiian Kids
COLORING BOOK

THIS BOOK WAS COLORED BY

....

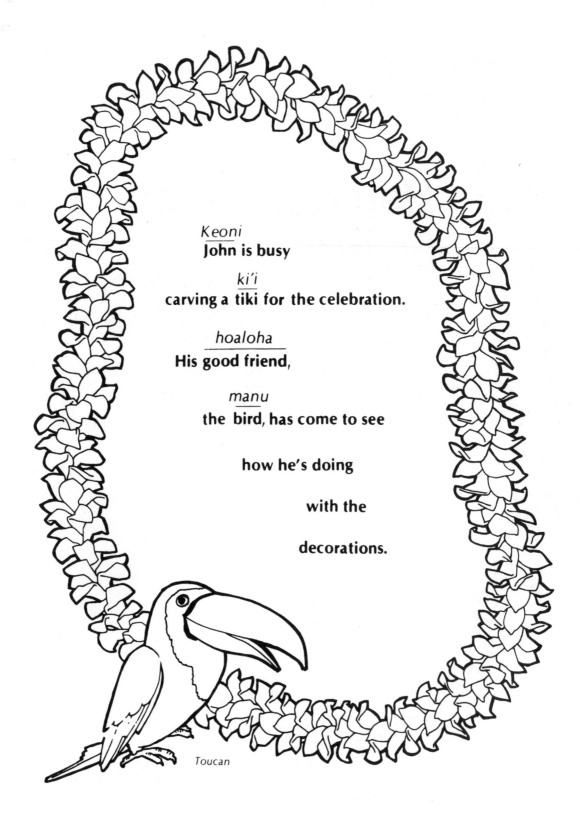

Keoni
John is busy

ki'i
carving a tiki for the celebration.

hoaloha
His good friend,

manu
the bird, has come to see

how he's doing

with the

decorations.

Toucan

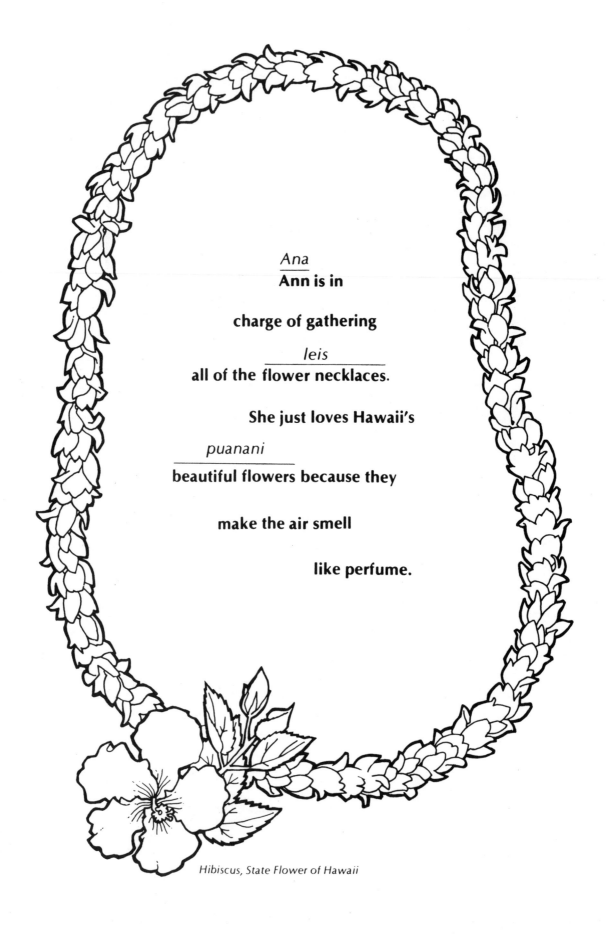

Ana
Ann is in

charge of gathering

leis
all of the flower necklaces.

She just loves Hawaii's

puanani
beautiful flowers because they

make the air smell

like perfume.

Hibiscus, State Flower of Hawaii

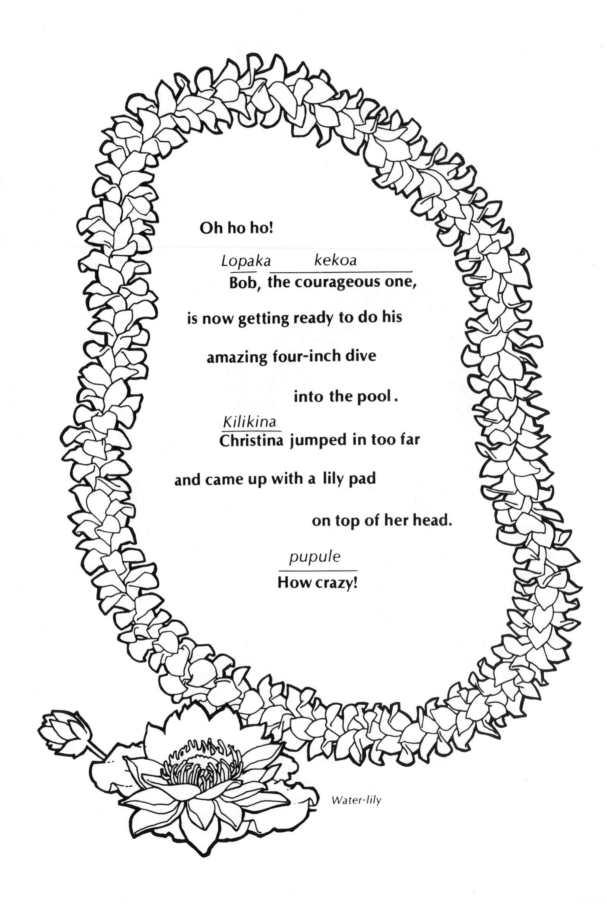

Oh ho ho!

Lopaka   *kekoa*
Bob, the courageous one,

is now getting ready to do his

amazing four-inch dive

into the pool.

Kilikina
Christina jumped in too far

and came up with a lily pad

on top of her head.

pupule
How crazy!

Water-lily

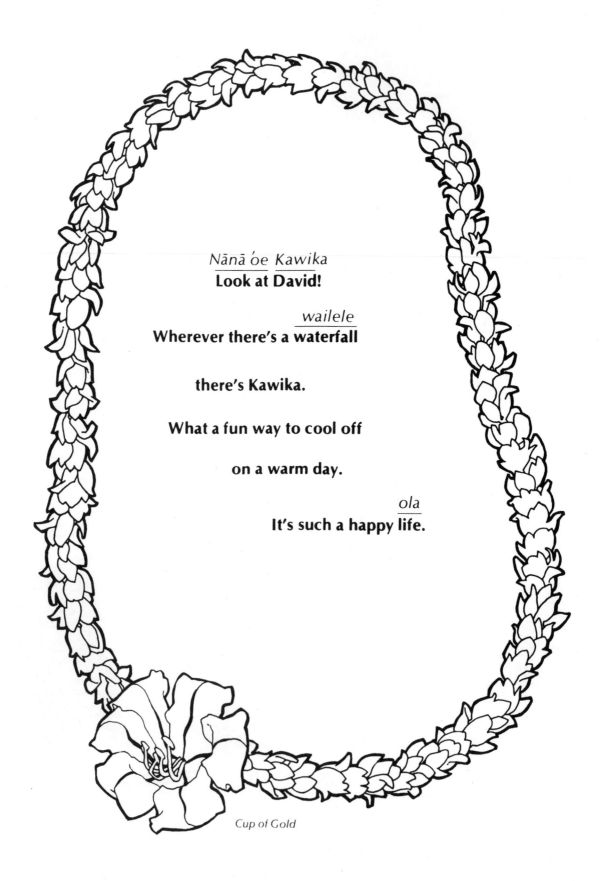

Nānā ʻoe Kawika
Look at David!

wailele
Wherever there's a waterfall

there's Kawika.

What a fun way to cool off

on a warm day.

ola
It's such a happy life.

Cup of Gold

Bird of Paradise

Yoo hoo, here she

Pilipo
comes. Phillip thought

he had the pool all to

Papela
himself, but Barbara

found him. Where there's

wainani
beautiful water there's a

way.

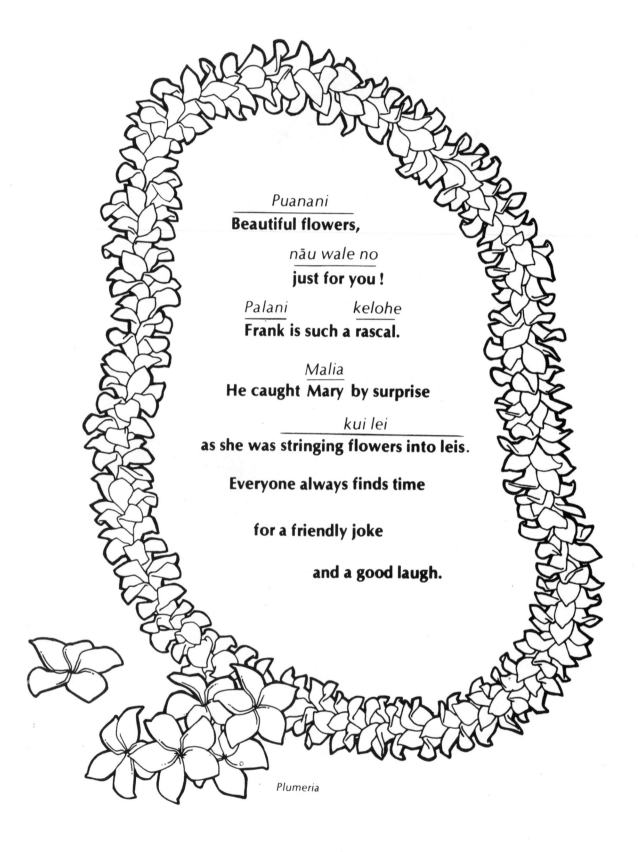

Puanani
Beautiful flowers,

nāu wale no
just for you !

Palani   *kelohe*
Frank is such a rascal.

Malia
He caught Mary by surprise

kui lei
as she was stringing flowers into leis.

Everyone always finds time

for a friendly joke

and a good laugh.

Plumeria

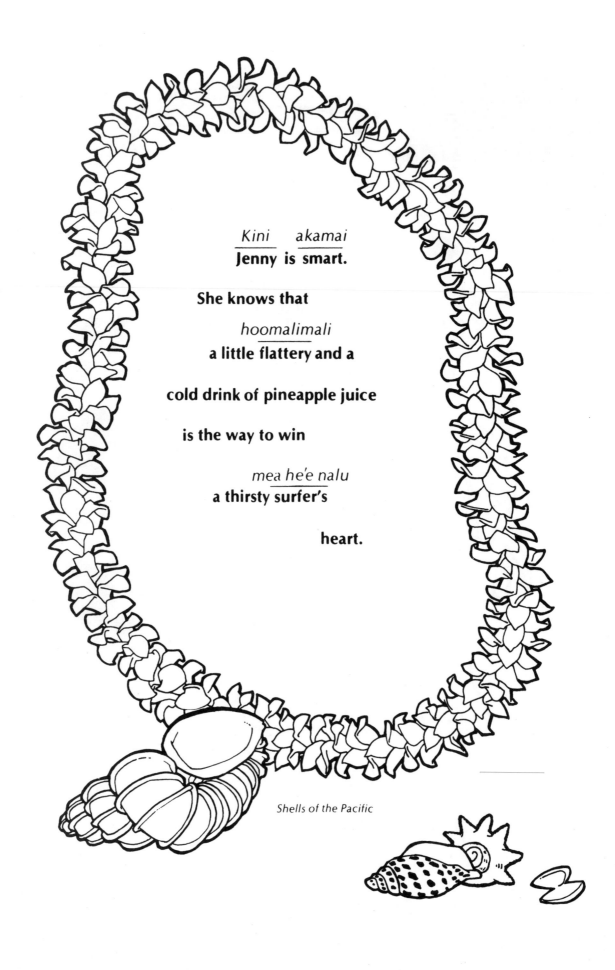

Kini   *akamai*
Jenny is smart.

She knows that

hoomalimali
a little flattery and a

cold drink of pineapple juice

is the way to win

mea he'e nalu
a thirsty surfer's

heart.

Shells of the Pacific

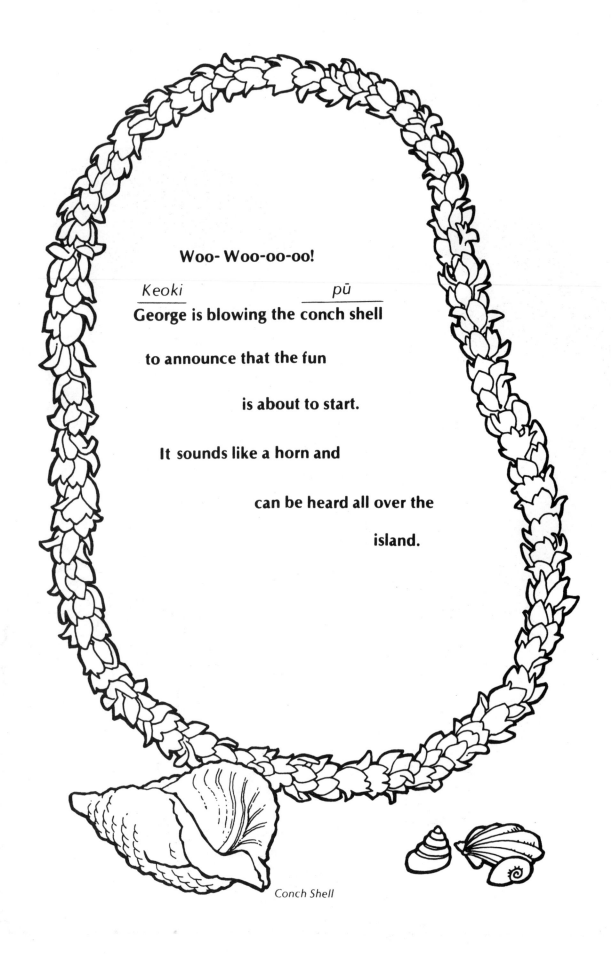

Woo- Woo-oo-oo!

Keoki   _pū_

George is blowing the conch shell

to announce that the fun

is about to start.

It sounds like a horn and

can be heard all over the

island.

Conch Shell

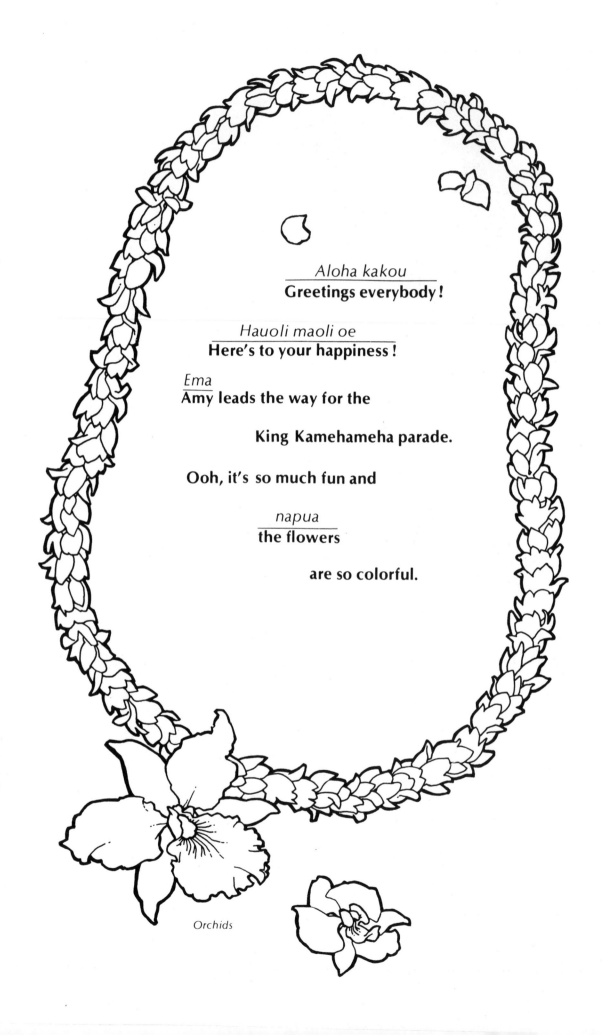

Aloha kakou
Greetings everybody!

Hauoli maoli oe
Here's to your happiness!

Ema
Amy leads the way for the

King Kamehameha parade.

Ooh, it's so much fun and

napua
the flowers

are so colorful.

Orchids

ATTENTION! Here is King Kamehameha the Great.

Analu
(But it's really only Andrew.)

What a grand

Pekelo
day it is for little **Peter.**

He was chosen to carry

kahili
the standard of royalty

for the king. How very proud

mua
he is to be first.

Torch Ginger

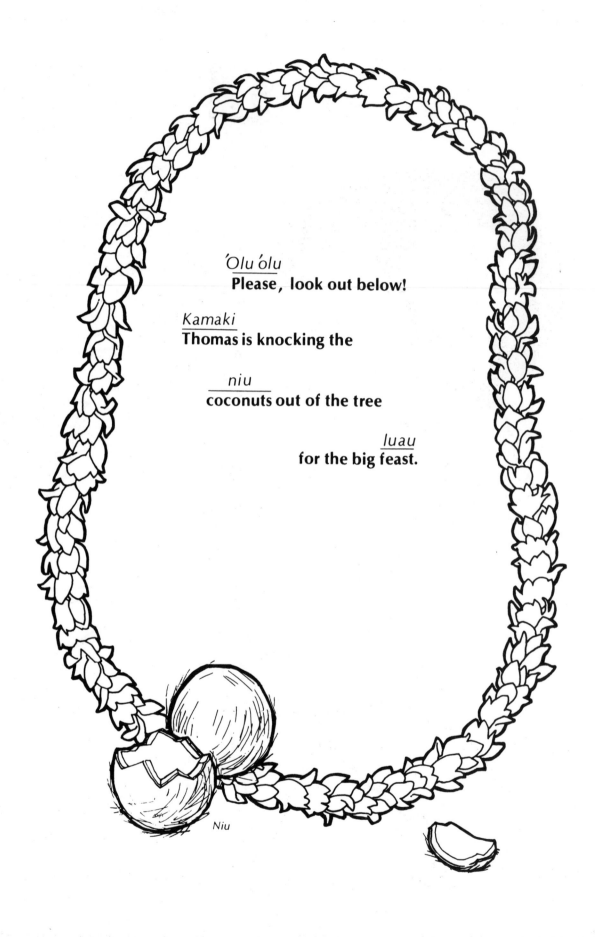

ʻOluʻolu
Please, look out below!

Kamaki
Thomas is knocking the

niu
coconuts out of the tree

luau
for the big feast.

Niu

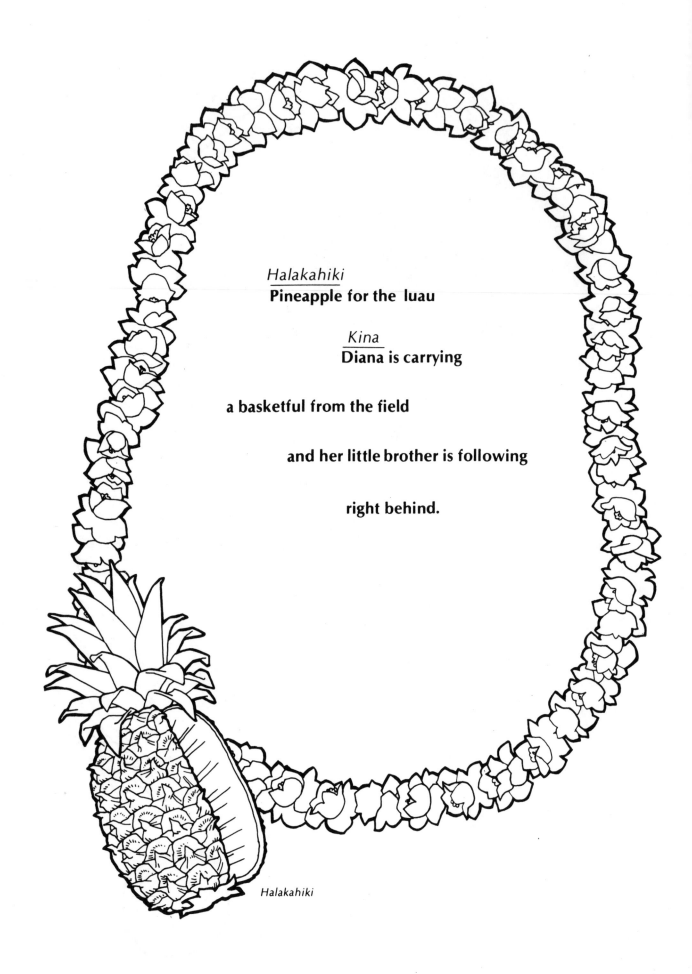

Halakahiki
Pineapple for the luau

Kina
Diana is carrying

a basketful from the field

and her little brother is following

right behind.

Halakahiki

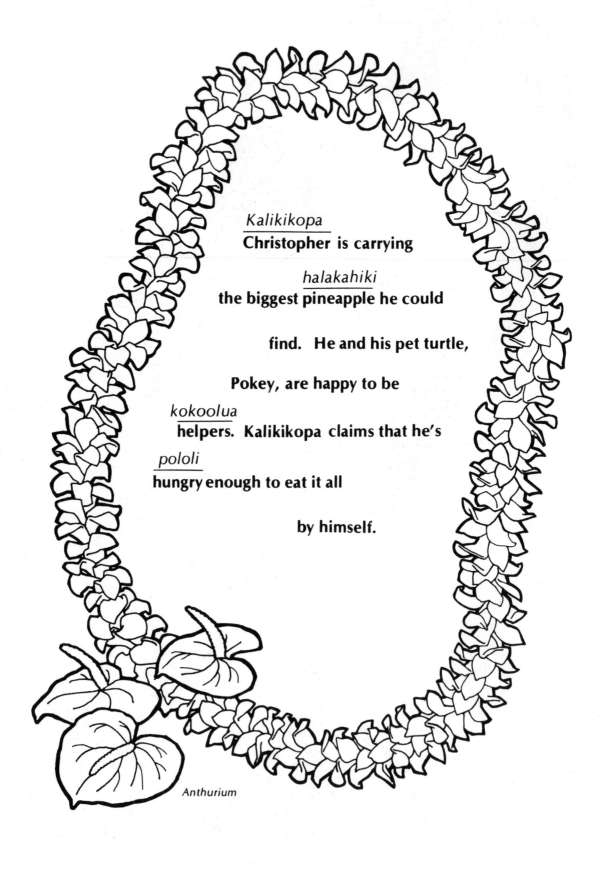

Kalikikopa
Christopher is carrying

halakahiki
the biggest pineapple he could

find.   He and his pet turtle,

Pokey, are happy to be

kokoolua
helpers. Kalikikopa claims that he's

pololi
hungry enough to eat it all

by himself.

Anthurium

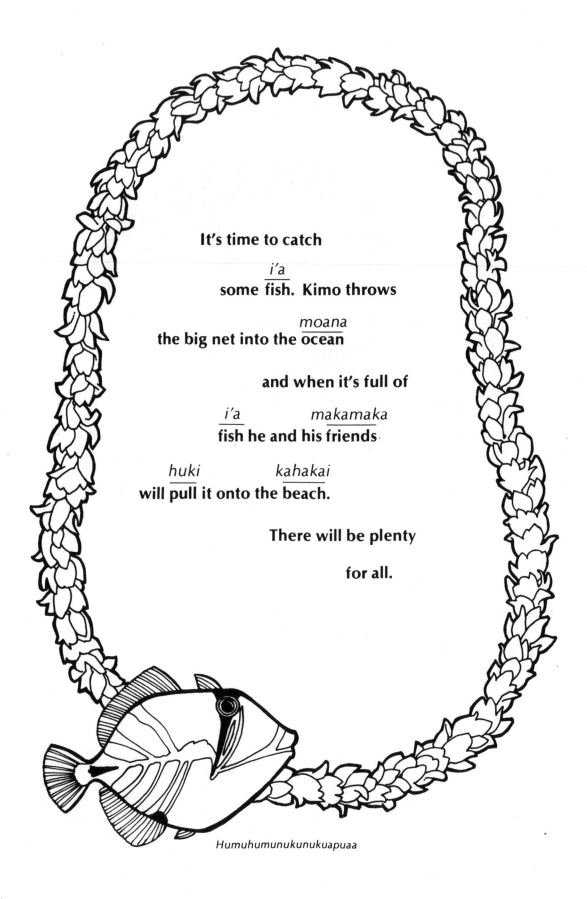

It's time to catch

i'a
some fish. Kimo throws

moana
the big net into the ocean

and when it's full of

i'a   *makamaka*
fish he and his friends

huki   *kahakai*
will pull it onto the beach.

There will be plenty

for all.

Humuhumunukunukuapuaa

Naneki
Nancy is

carefully spreading ti leaves

on the ground to

make a place for all

mai'a   *Maleko*
those bananas that Mark

has picked for

the party.

mai'a

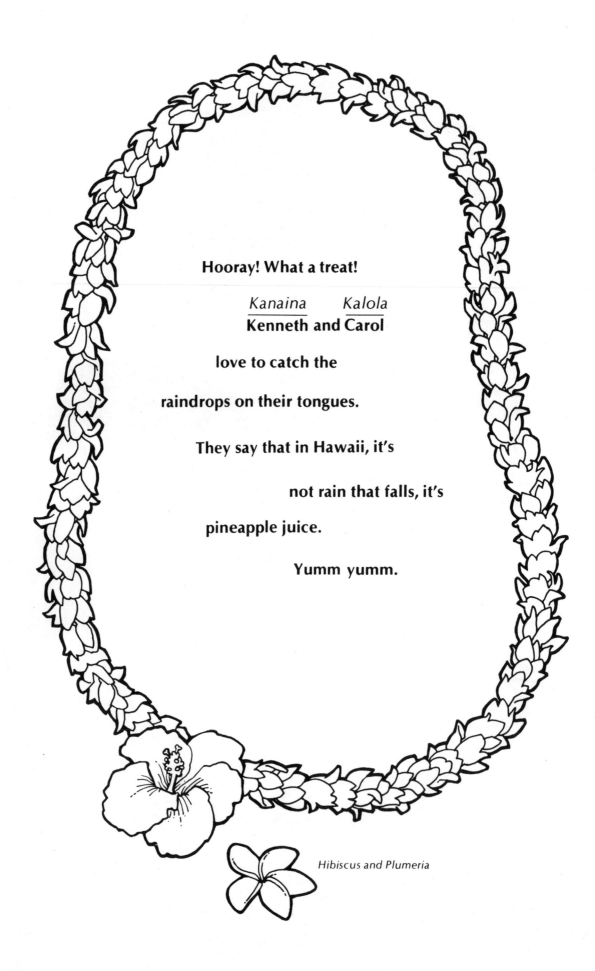

Hooray! What a treat!

Kanaina   *Kalola*
Kenneth and **Carol**

love to catch the

raindrops on their tongues.

They say that in Hawaii, it's

not rain that falls, it's

pineapple juice.

Yumm yumm.

Hibiscus and Plumeria

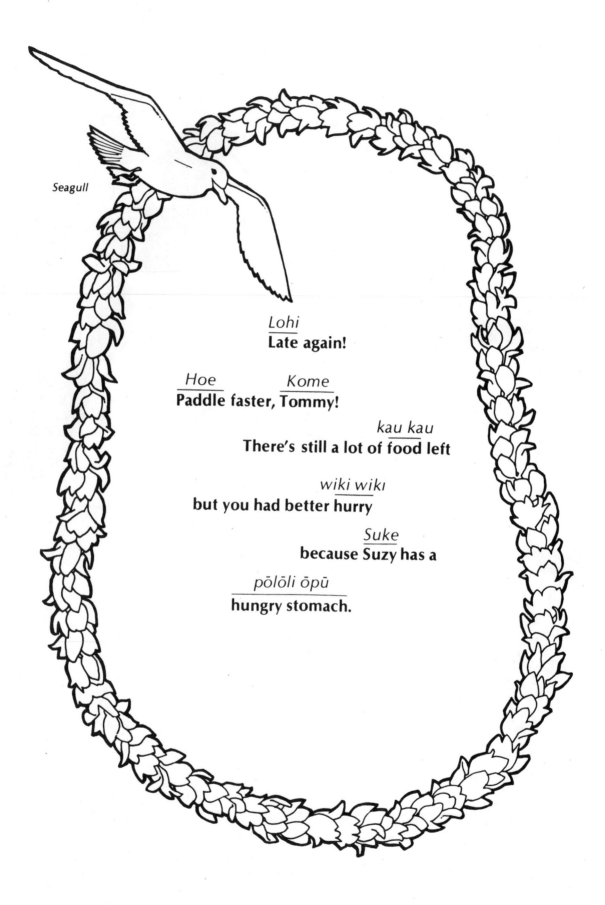

Seagull

Lohi
Late again!

Hoe   *Kome*
Paddle faster, Tommy!

kau kau
There's still a lot of food left

wiki wiki
but you had better hurry

Suke
because Suzy has a

pōlōli ōpū
hungry stomach.

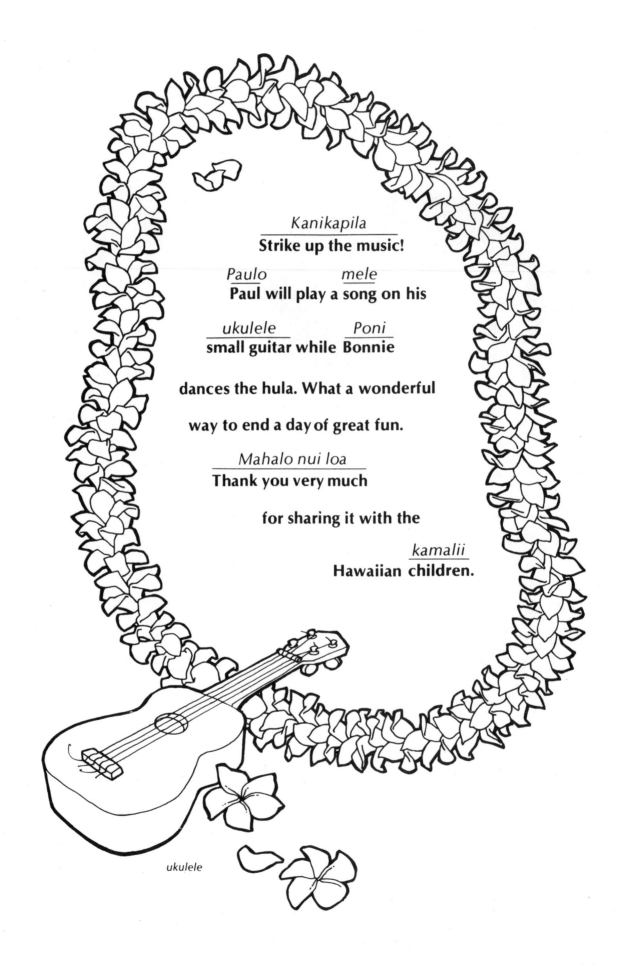

Kanikapila
Strike up the music!

Paulo   *mele*
Paul will play a song on his

ukulele   *Poni*
small guitar while Bonnie

dances the hula. What a wonderful

way to end a day of great fun.

Mahalo nui loa
Thank you very much

for sharing it with the

kamalii
Hawaiian children.

ukulele